Whispers of Life

Poems from the Heart

Dhanashree Nawale

BookLeaf Publishing

India | USA | UK

To the moments that shape us—

the quiet mornings, the stormy nights,

the laughter shared, and the tears shed.

To those who see beauty in the ordinary,

find strength in the struggles,

and embrace the journey of life with open hearts.

This book is for you.

May these words echo your own stories

*and bring solace, inspiration, and a touch of
magic.*

Acknowledgments

This book would not have been possible without the love, support, and inspiration of so many people who have touched my life in countless ways.

First and foremost, I thank my family, whose unwavering belief in me has been my greatest strength. Your encouragement has been the light that guided me through every step of this journey.

To my friends, who have been my sounding board, my cheerleaders, and my quiet supporters—thank you for listening, for understanding, and for inspiring me with your own beautiful stories of life.

A special thanks to the readers who find meaning in these words. Your connection to this work is what breathes life into these poems.

To the moments—both joyous and challenging—that have shaped me and this book: thank you for teaching me the lessons I needed to learn.

Lastly, I am deeply grateful to the creators of the art, literature, and music that have nourished my soul and sparked my creativity along the way.
This book is a reflection of all the love, learning, and beauty I have encountered. To everyone who has been part of this journey, whether directly or indirectly—thank you, from the bottom of my heart.

With endless gratitude,
Dhanashree Sumit Nawale

Preface

Life is a tapestry of emotions, woven with threads of joy, sorrow, love, and reflection. Each day presents a new verse, a fleeting moment that adds to the poem of our existence. This book is my humble attempt to capture those moments—the extraordinary in the ordinary, the whispers of the heart, and the stories hidden in plain sight.
The poems within these pages were born from my own experiences, as well as the world around me. They explore the beauty of human connection, the resilience of the spirit, and the lessons we learn as we navigate this journey called life.
As you turn these pages, my hope is that you'll find a piece of yourself in the words—a memory rekindled, a feeling validated, or a new perspective unveiled. Poetry has a way of speaking directly to the soul, and if even one line resonates with you, my purpose in writing this book will be fulfilled.

Let this collection be a companion on your journey, reminding you that life, with all its ups and downs, is a poem waiting to be written.

With gratitude and love,
Dhanashree Sumit Nawale

The Garden Of Childhood

The days of sunlit skies,
Where laughter soared and time would fly,
Barefoot races through fields of green,
A world of wonder, a timeless dream.
The scent of rain on summer air,
The thrill of swings that touched the rare,
Sticky fingers from stolen treats,
Echoes of joy in crowded streets.
Hide and seek 'til the stars would gleam,
Building castles in a muddy stream,
Every bruise a badge of pride,
Each adventure a world inside.
The whispered secrets, pinky swears,
Carefree hearts with no despairs,
A simple world of boundless glee,
Where every shadow was a mystery.
Now, I close my eyes to find,
That golden realm etched in my mind,
Oh, happy childhood, pure and true,
Forever a part of all I do.

The Ties That Time Can't Fade

In hallways filled with endless chatter,
Where giggles danced and notebooks scattered,
Bonds were built, unplanned, unseen,
In classrooms bursting with dreams between.
Whispers shared in the quiet of class,
Passing notes that made the time pass,
Lunchbox trades and secret plans,
A web of friendship spun by hands.
The playground echoed with joyous cheer,
Unspoken promises held us near,
Every game, every daring feat,
Bound us closer, heart to beat.
Through exams, shared cheers, and fleeting fights,
Late-night calls and endless writes,
We grew together, side by side,
In those golden years, we'd confide.
Though time may stretch and paths may part,
These memories stay within my heart,
For school friendships are a sacred thread,
A lifelong song in words unsaid.
Here's to the friends who shaped my youth,
To their laughter, their love, their simple truth,
Though miles may lie, though years may change,
The ties we share will still remain.

Skyborn Dreams

The boundless dreams of a child's bright mind,
A canvas of wonder, where stars align,
Where every thought takes wings to soar,
And every path opens an endless door.
Today a cricketer, bat in hand,
Tomorrow a hero to lead the land,
A scientist cracking the universe's code,
Or a painter crafting life's vibrant ode.
"I'll be an astronaut," the heart declares,
"Touching the moon with a million stares,"
"Or a pilot, high above the clouds,
Guiding the sky with a fearless vow."
A doctor, a teacher, a rock star's fame,
A fire-fighter, daring and brave by name,
Each ambition, a story of might,
Born in the magic of childhood's light.
There's no horizon too far, too wide,
No dream too wild to keep inside,
For a child's heart knows no constraints,
A limitless world their spirit paints.
Let us cherish these dreams, untamed and free,
For in their eyes lies infinity,
A reminder that once, we too believed,
In the impossible, joyfully conceived.

Fields of Gold and Bruised Knees

Life was a game on the dusty ground,
Where laughter and cheers would always resound,
A world of play, so wild, so free,
Where scraped-up knees were a badge to see.
The clang of bells, the dash to the field,
With nothing but joy as our only shield,
A cricket bat, a football's flight,
Under the sun's golden, endless light.
The thrill of running, the chase, the fall,
The triumph of scoring, the victory call,
Bruises and cuts were marks of pride,
Proof of the battles fought outside.
School sports days with flags held high,
Relays and races that made us fly,
The crowd would cheer, the anthem would play,
As we chased glory on those fleeting days.
No worries then, no burdens to bear,
Just the wind in our hair, the cool, fresh air,
Our world was the court, the track, the ball,
And in those moments, we had it all.
Oh, to return to those carefree days,
Where life was a game, and we loved its ways,
For in every injury, in every cheer,
Lies a memory we hold most dear.

The Flame Jumper

She stood at the edge, the world below,
A girl with courage, a heart aglow,
The fire roared, the crowd held tight,
She was a beacon, fierce and bright.
The first to dive, from heights so high,
With flames reflecting in her eyes,
A leap of faith, a fearless flight,
Her spirit soared, a dazzling sight.
The school erupted in endless cheers,
She faced her challenge, quelled her fears,
Her name was whispered, her story told,
A tale of bravery, fierce and bold.
Not just a dive, but a role profound,
In the martial arts show, she astound,
Kicks and stances, swift and true,
A warrior's grace in all she'd do.
She fought with skill, a blazing star,
Her strength and will surpassed by far,
The crowd admired her daring ways,
She basked in well-deserved praise.
That girl became a legend there,
Her fiery dive, her fearless flair,
An inspiration, her story stays,
A timeless tale of her shining days.

When Paths Divide

The bell tolls its final chime,
Marking the end of a golden time,
We pack our books, our laughter, our tears,
And step away from the cherished years.
Best friends bound by the strongest ties,
Now gaze at the world with heavy eyes,
For distance looms, a bittersweet fate,
As life pulls us through another gate.
The classroom walls, the familiar halls,
Echo with memories of whispered calls,
Of stolen jokes and shared dreams bright,
Now fading gently into the night.
One moves east, another west,
Each to follow their own life's quest,
But hearts resist what minds must bear,
For bonds like ours are ever rare.
Though cities rise to keep us apart,
You'll always live within my heart,
Each text, each call, a thread we weave,
To keep alive what we believe.
And when the miles feel too wide to cross,
I'll close my eyes and bear no loss,
For in my mind, we'll always stay,
Best friends forever, come what may.

So here's to us, to the love we keep,
To the promises carved so deep,
Though roads may part and years may fly,
Our friendship's flame will never die.

Roots of Steel, Wings of Fire

She walked into the city's gleaming light,
A small-town girl, a fearless sight,
With dreams that soared and heart untamed,
A quiet strength, her soul proclaimed.
No whispers followed, no mocking stares,
For her presence spoke, her confidence rare,
She didn't seek to blend or hide,
She owned the moment, stride by stride.
In the bustling halls of a college new,
Where the world seemed vast, horizons grew,
She wasn't lost; she wasn't shy,
Her spirit bold, her gaze held high.
Her roots were deep, her pride was clear,
No need for approval, no space for fear,
She didn't conform; she didn't bend,
For she was her own, not needing to pretend.
In every debate, her voice was strong,
Her words like a melody, sharp and long,
She led with grace, she stood her ground,
Her courage echoed, a steady sound.
They didn't mock; they stood in awe,
Of a girl who lived by her own law,
She fit in not by changing hue,
But by being herself, authentic and true.

A small-town star in a city's embrace,
Her fearless heart lit every space,
For she taught the world a lesson clear:
True strength is born when you hold yourself
dear.

Unbreakable Threads

In the chaos of life, through joy and strife,
There's a bond that feels like the essence of life,
A sibling's love, both fierce and kind,
A treasure of the heart, forever entwined.
From childhood days of endless play,
To whispered secrets tucked away,
They've seen it all—your smiles, your tears,
Your greatest joys, your deepest fears.
Fights over toys, and who gets the best,
A tug-of-war that never rests,
Yet, in the end, when trouble's near,
They're the first to wipe your tears.
A look, a laugh, a shared inside joke,
A language spoken, though no words are woke,
Their presence steady, like the earth and sky,
An anchor strong when storms are nigh.
Through distant miles or years apart,
They live forever within your heart,
A sibling's bond—no thread can sever,
A tie that holds through time, forever.
So here's to the ones who've known you best,
Your silent heroes, your lifelong nest,
For in their love, there's no pretend,
A sibling's bond—the truest friend.

Wings of Trust

They never raised their voice to the sky,
But held out their hands and let us fly,
With gentle words, their wisdom grew,
A garden of trust in which we flew.
No chains of fear, no walls of doubt,
Their love was calm, a whispered shout,
They guided, they listened, they let us lead,
Sowing the seeds for what we'd need.
They trusted our steps, both sure and unsure,
Believing our hearts would find what's pure,
In every fall, in every rise,
They saw the world through our eager eyes.
Rules were soft, but values were clear,
Freedom with love, not ruled by fear,
They taught us strength in tender ways,
A bond of respect that always stays.
From painted skies to dreams so wide,
They stood by us, a steady guide,
Not as judges, but as friends so dear,
Cheering us on year after year.
Now as we soar in skies unbound,
Their gentle whispers still resound,
For parents who trust and set us free,
Are the winds beneath the wings of eternity.

Pillars of Love

In the ebb and flow of life's vast sea,
One anchor holds steadfastly—
My family, my rock, my guiding light,
Through darkest storms and brightest nights.
When I stumble, they lend their hand,
A steady force, a gentle stand,
Through every phase, through every trial,
They lift me up with a heartfelt smile.
Their faith in me, a boundless grace,
A warmth no hardship can replace,
In every triumph, they cheer with pride,
In every failure, they're by my side.
They teach, they listen, they understand,
A fortress built with love's own hand,
With laughter shared and tears consoled,
Their strength is a treasure, precious than gold.
Through childhood dreams to grown-up fears,
Through fleeting joys and lasting tears,
Their love remains a constant star,
Guiding me, no matter how far.
To my family, my heart's true home,
In their embrace, I'm never alone,
With gratitude deep, I humbly say,
Thank you for lighting my every day.

Sunshine

I met him not in grandeur's glow,
But in the quiet where true hearts show,
A soul so humble, kind, and true,
The kind I dreamt of but never knew.
His words, like whispers, calm and kind,
A depth of love so rare to find,
In his eyes, the gentlest hue,
A mirror of skies, serene and blue.
He didn't boast, nor sought the crown,
Yet his presence lifted my world from the ground,
With every smile, he built a space,
Where love could flourish, filled with grace.
He saw my soul, not just my face,
In his heart, I found my place,
No pretense, no masks, no need to pretend,
A partner, a lover, my truest friend.
His touch was warm, a silent vow,
To stand by me through then and now,
A true gentleman, steadfast and strong,
With him, my life feels like a song.
And as the days weave into years,
Through shared laughter and quiet tears,
I know in him, my heart has found,
A love eternal, deeply profound.

Oh, how grateful my soul remains,
For the one who healed, who broke my chains,
He is my partner, my life, my muse,
The love of my life I'd never refuse.

Eternal Grace of Shri Krishna

Oh Shri Krishna, keeper of the eternal tune,
With your flute's melody under the moon,
You guide my heart with a gentle hand,
Through life's rough seas to promised land.
In your gaze, the cosmos unfolds,
A thousand tales your smile holds,
Protector, friend, a love so pure,
In your presence, all wounds endure.
Thank you for the love you impart,
For planting joy within my heart,
For every blessing, seen and unseen,
And the peace you bring, soft and serene.
When storms arise and shadows fall,
Your name is my anchor, my all in all,
You carry my burdens, my fears you erase,
Filling my soul with boundless grace.
Through every moment, through every prayer,
Your divine love is always there,
Teaching me faith, showing me light,
Even in darkness, you shine so bright.
Oh Shri Krishna, my gratitude flows,
Like a river of devotion that endlessly grows,
For your love, eternal and divine,
Forever, I am yours, and you are mine.

Miles from Home, Dreams in Sight

I packed my bags with trembling hands,
Left behind familiar lands,
A heart heavy with love's embrace,
To chase a dream, to find my place.
The nights grew long, the silence loud,
Amidst the city's bustling crowd,
A lonely soul, yet fire within,
To carve a path, to rise, to win.
The struggle bore its daily test,
Of sleepless nights and endless quests,
But through the toil, I heard their cheer,
My family's faith forever near.
Their voices echoed across the miles,
Their love my strength, their hopes my smile,
In every setback, in every fall,
Their belief stood strong, their pride stood tall.
Each milestone reached, each lesson learned,
Through trials faced and bridges burned,
I grew, I soared, I found my way,
Though far from home, I lived each day.
But oh, the ache, the wistful tears,
For moments missed through fleeting years,
A sibling's laugh, a parent's touch,

The simple things I craved so much.
Yet in my heart, I hold them close,
Their love, the anchor I need the most,
For every step, their dreams align,
My journey's theirs, their strength is mine.
And one fine day, when dreams are done,
I'll return to them, my battles won,
With stories of growth and struggles endured,
A bond unbroken, a love assured.

The Dance of Shadows and Light

Life sways between joy and pain,
A shifting rhythm, sun and rain,
Moments of laughter, tears that stream,
A bittersweet and endless dream.
Sadness whispers in the night,
A shadow soft, a fleeting fright,
Yet even in the darkest skies,
A spark of hope begins to rise.
Happiness, a fleeting glow,
A gift we cherish, yet we know,
It comes and goes, a gentle guest,
Leaving memories to hold and rest.
But every sunrise paints the skies,
With golden hues that promise life,
A new beginning, fresh and bright,
To chase away the fading night.
For storms may come, and storms may pass,
But fields will bloom from barren grass,
In every sorrow, a lesson hides,
In every joy, the heart abides.
So dance with both, the light and shade,
For life is a symphony beautifully made,
And through it all, the soul will find,
Hope in the heart, forever enshrined.

A Bond Beyond Words

There is a love so pure, so rare,
Unspoken, yet it lingers there,
A quiet flame, a steady glow,
A gift of the heart that few may know.
No need for words, no need for claims,
It simply exists, untouched by names,
Free from anger, free from demands,
A bond unbroken, like timeless sands.
She moves through life, unbound, carefree,
And in her joy, I find my glee,
No expectation tethers this tie,
It soars like a bird in an open sky.
Her laughter feels like the morning sun,
A warmth that stays when the day is done,
Her smallest triumph, her every fall,
Are moments cherished, the greatest of all.
To love without want, to give without need,
Is a joy that grows like a planted seed,
No grudges linger, no harshness stays,
Only endless care in infinite ways.
It's not for reward, not for a sign,
But for the peace that love defines,
A bond so simple, yet profound,
A love like this is where grace is found.

Journeys Beyond Roads

A trip begins with a single stride,
A call to wander, a world to confide,
Through winding paths and skies so wide,
Adventure whispers, "Come and try."
Each step unfolds a lesson anew,
In mountains high or seas so blue,
The art of patience, the gift of grace,
The joy of finding a stranger's embrace.
Lost in alleys, maps torn apart,
We learn to trust the beating heart,
To let go of plans, to flow with time,
To see the beauty in life's design.
The thrill of cliffs, the rush of streams,
Awaken the courage to chase our dreams,
For every journey teaches the soul,
To face the unknown and make it whole.
The laughter shared, the stories told,
In camps beneath the starlit cold,
Forge bonds that time may never fray,
Memories etched in the heart to stay.
And when we return to our routine,
We carry the strength from all we've seen,
For every trip, both near and far,
Leaves us braver than we were.

So pack your bag, embrace the call,
Life's greatest lessons await us all,
In every journey, there lies a part,
That shapes our mind and fills our heart.

The Path to Inner Peace

Amid the noise, the endless chase,
Lies a quiet, sacred space,
Where peace resides, a gentle stream,
A tranquil heart, a timeless dream.
Life may pull with trials vast,
Storms of the future, echoes of the past,
But the soul whispers, calm and clear,
"Come inward, child, find solace here."
Through meditation, the stillness grows,
A seed of light that softly glows,
Each breath a step, each thought released,
Toward a haven of inner peace.
No need for answers, no need for more,
The self contains a boundless shore,
In silence, truths begin to rise,
Unseen beneath the worldly guise.
The spiritual path, a winding trail,
With lessons rich when doubts assail,
It teaches love; it teaches grace,
And shows the soul its rightful place.
The stars above, the earth below,
Remind us of the flow we know,
Connected threads, a cosmic art,
Binding the universe to our hearts.

So pause, let go, and simply be,
Embrace the stillness, wild and free,
For peace is not a place you find,
But a journey within the quiet mind.

Threads of Unstoppable Grace

In the tapestry of life's winding ways,
There shines a bond that brightens days,
A friendship forged, so strong, so true,
A sisterhood built from hearts that grew.
With shared secrets and endless talks,
Laughter echoing through midnight walks,
A world of comfort, a safe embrace,
Where love and trust find their place.
They lift each other when skies turn gray,
With gentle words, they light the way,
No judgment clouds, no masks to wear,
Just honest hearts that deeply care.
Through every triumph, every fall,
They cheer the loudest, they catch it all,
In their strength, there's beauty untold,
A bond more precious than the rarest gold.
They celebrate dreams, both big and small,
And stand together when shadows call,
For girl friendships are wild and free,
A dance of spirits, eternally.
Like the moon and stars, they shine so bright,
Guiding each other through the darkest night,
A sisterhood of love, a treasure divine,
Forever cherished, a lifeline.

The Allies at the Desk

In the hum of work, amidst the grind,
There shines a bond, one of a kind,
A friendship born in deadlines' race,
A steady hand, a smiling face.
Through endless meetings, tasks that drain,
They're the sunshine amid the rain,
With words of cheer on weary days,
And laughter that lights the darkest haze.
When stress mounts high and doubts take hold,
They lend their strength, their warmth, their gold,
A pep talk here, a coffee there,
A quiet moment that says, "I care."
They celebrate the smallest win,
The joy of goals reached deep within,
With clinking cups or simple cheer,
Their presence makes triumph sincere.
And when the lows come creeping near,
They're the voice that drowns the fear,
Lifting spirits with kindness shown,
Reminding you, you're not alone.
In the workplace maze, they're the guide,
The confidant who walks beside,
Turning work from a daily chore,
Into a place you value more.

To these friends, steadfast and true,
A heartfelt thanks for all you do,
For in your bond, there's endless grace,
A haven found in life's busy pace.

The Pulse of Progress

A spark of code, a wire's hum,
From simple roots, a world has come,
Technology, a force untamed,
Transforming lives, unbound, unclaimed.
From wheels of old to engines bright,
To screens that glow in endless light,
Each leap a marvel, each stride profound,
A symphony of ideas unbound.
The rise of AI, the data streams,
Machines that think and code dreams,
From virtual realms to skies explored,
Technology's march cannot be ignored.
It builds, it learns, it changes shape,
From labs of thought to wide escape,
Connecting hearts, yet widening gaps,
Bringing the world within our grasp.
Yet with this power comes a test,
To wield it wisely, to seek the best,
To balance growth with human care,
And nurture worlds that all can share.
For in its pace, its boundless flight,
Lies the future, dark and bright,
A tool of wonder, a force of might,
Guided well, it births the light.

So here we stand, on progress's brink,
With tech evolving as we think,
May we create with thoughtful hand,
A brighter world, a better land.

Partners in the Hustle

In the dance of dreams and daily grind,
Two hearts beat as one, aligned,
Through the chaos, the climb, the unknown race,
We find our strength in each other's grace.
Side by side, we build and strive,
Not just careers, but a life alive,
Through sleepless nights and weary days,
Your love is my light, my guiding blaze.
When the road gets rough and the stakes are high,
You're the voice that lifts me, the reason I try,
A cheerleader, a rock, my truest friend,
With you, every struggle feels easy to mend.
We hustle together, we dream as one,
Sharing the weight until the work is done,
Celebrating triumphs, big and small,
Unconditional love through it all.
You hold my hand when I start to doubt,
Reminding me what life's about,
Not just the goals, the things we achieve,
But the bond we share, the love we weave.
For in this hustle, we've come to see,
Our journey together is the key,
With you, my partner, my heart, my guide,
I find my home, no matter the stride.

So here's to us, to the life we create,
To love and dreams, to a shared fate,
For hustling together, we've come to know,
In each other's arms, we'll always grow.

The Inevitable Truth

In the cradle of dawn, a cry is heard,
A soul descends, wrapped in life's word.
The first breath taken, a spark of grace,
A fleeting glimpse of this earthly space.
Tiny hands clutch the threads of time,
Innocent hearts, untouched by the climb.
Yet etched in stars and whispered by skies,
Life's basic truth: one who is born dies.
The sun will rise, and seasons will change,
Moments of joy, a life's full range.
Love will bloom in a tender embrace,
Time will carve lines upon every face.
The heart will ache, and the tears will fall,
Yet beauty lingers through it all.
For every goodbye, a lesson lies,
That one who is born inevitably dies.
But death's not the end, just another door,
A path to realms unseen before.
What we leave behind, our love, our name,
The memories cherished, the unquenched flame.
So live with kindness, laugh without fear,
Hold close the ones you hold dear.
For life is a gift, a fleeting prize,
And one who is born truly never dies.

Lunar Inspiration

High above in the velvet sky,
The moon ascends, its gaze so shy.
Yet steadfast, bright, and ever whole,
It whispers dreams to every soul.
Through darkest nights, it softly gleams,
A beacon of hope, a keeper of dreams.
It shows us light when shadows grow,
A quiet guide to where we'll go.
It waxes, wanes, yet never hides,
Teaching patience with changing tides.
For every phase, a story unfolds,
A lesson in time, a strength that molds.
"Chase your dreams," it seems to say,
"Even stars bow to those who stay.
Reflect your light, though it may seem small,
For even a sliver can brighten it all."
The moon reminds, with every climb,
That goals are met with toil and time.
Its journey round the Earth so clear,
A silent vow, a voice sincere.
So when doubt looms and courage wanes,
Look to the moon, through windowpanes.
For in its glow, you'll find your way,
A quiet push to seize the day.

The Heart of Her Being

She rises with the sun, her heart aglow,
A nurturer, a force the world must know.
In her hands, she cradles life's fragile thread,
Her touch, a balm where hope has fled.
With tender grace, she mends and tends,
Her love, a circle that never ends.
She breathes life into every role,
A mother, a sister, a heart, a soul.
In the chaos of days, she stands so still,
Balancing dreams with unyielding will.
Her strength is silent, yet fierce and true,
She carries the weight of the world anew.
Her mind is a map, her heart a guide,
She builds bridges where divides reside.
Her laughter heals, her tears refine,
She is beauty incarnate, divine by design.
She's the keeper of stories, the weaver of dreams,
The quiet hero behind the scenes.
Her hands can nurture, her spirit can fight,
A beacon of love, a source of light.
Though unseen burdens may line her face,
She wears them with an unbroken grace.
A multitasker, a queen of her art,
She binds the world with the strings of her heart.

So here's to her—the nurturer supreme,
A warrior of life, a river, a stream.
Her beauty's not just in what you see,
But in the boundless depths of her humanity.

Ode to Coffee

In the quiet hush of morning's glow,
A fragrant warmth begins to flow.
Dark and rich, a liquid art,
Coffee stirs my weary heart.
From golden beans to velvet streams,
It fuels my thoughts, ignites my dreams.
Each sip a story, each cup a muse,
A ritual I'll never refuse.
The first taste, bold, a bitter-sweet,
Awakens my soul, a daily treat.
Its aroma dances, fills the air,
A moment of solace beyond compare.
Through hectic days and quiet nights,
It holds my hand, my soul ignites.
A friend in laughter, a balm in strife,
Coffee, you're the rhythm of life.
Latte, mocha, or espresso divine,
Each one whispers, "This time is mine."
A pause, a breath, a chance to be,
To savor life's simplicity.
Oh, coffee love, so deep, so true,
What would my world be without you?
A toast to you, my faithful brew,
Forever cherished, forever new.

A Mother's Care

In her arms, the world feels right,
A harbor safe in the darkest night.
Her touch, a balm, so soft, so warm,
A shield that guards against life's storm.
Her voice, a melody, calm and sweet,
Guides tiny steps with steady feet.
In her eyes, a universe glows,
Where love unspoken quietly flows.
She mends the tears that life may bring,
Turns pain to hope with a gentle swing.
Her care, a fire that never wanes,
Through joys and sorrows, losses, gains.
Her hands, though tired, never rest,
Forever giving, always their best.
Her heart beats in rhythms profound,
A love so pure, eternally unbound.
She sees the dreams we're too shy to share,
Nurtures them with tender care.
Her sacrifices, silent and deep,
A treasure of love we'll always keep.
Oh, mother's care, a sacred art,
A wellspring flowing from her heart.
In her embrace, life's meaning is found,
A bond unbroken, forever profound.

Her Two Worlds

Monday dawns with a heavy sigh,
A suitcase packed, a whispered goodbye.
She boards the train, her heart in tow,
To a city where dreams and duty grow.
Through bustling halls and endless calls,
She builds her life within these walls.
A working woman, fierce and true,
Juggling roles the world never knew.
The weekdays blur, a ceaseless grind,
But her family's love is etched in mind.
Each late-night chat, each morning text,
A lifeline strong, her soul's reflex.
Come Friday evening, her heart takes flight,
Back to her haven, her guiding light.
With every hug, the world feels whole,
Their love, the balm that heals her soul.
Her children's laughter, her partner's cheer,
Erase the miles, dissolve the fear.
In their arms, she finds her place,
A weekend sanctuary, a warm embrace.
They know her strength, her tireless fight,
To balance it all, to make it right.
Their faith in her, their endless care,
Is what she breathes, her steady air.

Through two cities, two lives she weaves,
Her dreams and love in balance she grieves.
Yet her heart beats strong, her spirit high,
For her family's love is her northern sky.
So here she stands, unbroken, proud,
A woman of purpose, a soul unbowed.
Through work and home, she carves her way,
Fueled by love, her guiding ray.

Across the Screens

The day winds down, the world grows still,
The stars emerge beyond the hill.
But hearts ignite in a warm embrace,
As siblings gather, face to face.
Across the screens, their laughter flows,
A timeless bond that ever grows.
Different cities, yet close they stay,
A digital bridge for hearts at play.
"Tell me your day," the eldest starts,
Their words like threads that mend their hearts.
Jokes are shared and stories spun,
Echoes of love from everyone.
The youngest grins, a playful tease,
Their banter floats with casual ease.
Memories bloom, both old and new,
A tapestry rich, a love so true.
Each pause is filled with silent care,
Though miles apart, they're always there.
For in this call, the world feels small,
Their voices build an unseen hall.
A moment brief, yet deeply sweet,
Where distant hearts in rhythm meet.
Though scattered far, they're never alone,
For family's love transcends the phone.

The call ends with a tender cheer,
"Goodnight," they say, "I'm always near."
And as they sleep in separate skies,
The bond remains, it never dies.

The Quest for the One

In the vast expanse of hearts unknown,
A lonely soul seeks its own.
A partner to share life's gentle fire,
A bond of love, a shared desire.
Yet paths are tangled, the way unsure,
Through smiles and promises, none seem pure.
In a world of faces, so many to see,
How do you find who's meant to be?
A heart that listens, a soul that cares,
A love that grows through life's repairs.
But the search can weary, the road feel long,
When whispers of doubt replace love's song.
For true connection is hard to find,
It's more than beauty, more than mind.
It's trust that blooms through trials faced,
A love unhurried, steady, and chaste.
The wrong ones teach, the right ones stay,
Yet finding them takes patience's way.
A partner who sees beyond the veil,
Through storms of life, they'll never pale.
So wander on, though the journey's steep,
Let hope and faith your spirit keep.
For in the dance of stars above,
Awaits your partner, your destined love.

And when they come, you'll know it's true,
For the world will glow in a brighter hue.
The search, though hard, will seem worthwhile,
When you find the one who makes you smile.

The Commute Chronicles

The morning sun begins its climb,
I mount my bike, right on time.
Helmet snug, a steady grip,
Through the city's veins, I make my trip.
The hum of engines fills the air,
A symphony of chaos everywhere.
Cars and buses, a crawling tide,
Through honking horns, I deftly glide.
The lanes are narrow, the rush immense,
The weaving game, a practiced sense.
A moment here, a space to claim,
Navigating through this daily game.
The wind whispers past, a fleeting cheer,
A reminder of freedom, always near.
Though the traffic clogs, the journey slows,
My two wheels dance where the chaos flows.
Red lights halt, the minutes crawl,
But patience builds amidst it all.
A passerby grins, a child waves by,
Little joys as the world rushes by.
Through crowded streets, I find my way,
A rider's rhythm, day by day.
For amidst the traffic's endless fight,
There's solace in this morning rite.

At last, I see my destination near,
The chaos fades; the path grows clear.
I park my bike, my journey done,
Another day's battle, another one won.
Through traffic's maze, I've learned to steer,
With grit and grace, and a mind sincere.
For life's like riding, through stop and start,
A test of balance, a work of heart.

White Canvas

From the heavens, soft and slow,
Falls the magic, pure as snow.
Each flake unique, a tiny art,
A gentle kiss upon the heart.
The world transforms, a canvas white,
A silent hymn in the hush of night.
Trees wear crowns of frosty grace,
A tranquil charm in every space.
The air turns crisp, the earth feels new,
As winter's blanket hides the view.
Footsteps crunch on powdered ground,
A soothing rhythm, a peaceful sound.
Children laugh as snowballs fly,
Their giggles mingling with the sky.
A snowman rises, proud and tall,
A fleeting joy that warms us all.
Yet in this chill, a warmth takes hold,
A fire within, defying the cold.
For snow reminds, in its quiet way,
Beauty lingers, though skies are gray.
So let it fall, this winter's song,
A fleeting wonder, but never wrong.
For in the snow's soft, sacred dance,
The world finds peace, a fleeting chance.

The Joy She Brings

A cry of life, so soft, so sweet,
Tiny hands, tiny feet.
The world is brighter, the air is light,
A girl is born, a family's delight.
She brings a spark, a radiant glow,
A love so pure, it seems to grow.
Her laughter echoes through every hall,
Her smile, the greatest gift of all.
She's the morning sun, a gentle breeze,
A melody that puts hearts at ease.
With every step, she lights the way,
A treasure cherished every day.
Her curious eyes, her playful cheer,
Turn every moment to one held dear.
She weaves her magic, her innocent charm,
A soothing balm, a healing calm.
She teaches strength, she shows us grace,
A quiet power in her embrace.
Through her, the world feels whole,
Her presence a balm for every soul.
The house she fills with endless mirth,
A girl, a blessing of infinite worth.
For in her smile, the family sees,
The promise of love, life's sweetest ease.

So celebrate her, this wondrous light,
A girl child's love, a family's delight.
For she is joy, hope, and pride,
A gift of life, love magnified.

Shri Krishna: The Eternal Flute

Upon the banks of Yamuna's flow,
Where the fragrant Kadamba trees grow,
Dances a youth with a radiant glow,
Shri Krishna, the world's eternal show.
With a peacock feather in his crown,
And a flute that melts all sorrow down,
He charms the hearts of every soul,
In love divine, he makes us whole.
The Gopis' whispers, the cows' soft calls,
Echo through Vrindavan's walls.
His laughter rings, his footsteps trace,
A path of joy, a divine embrace.
In Kurukshetra, where dharma stood,
He spoke the Gita, wise and good.
A guide to truth, a path to grace,
To every seeker, he shows his face.
Oh Krishna, dark as the monsoon sky,
With lotus eyes that never lie,
You play your Leela, vast and deep,
Awake in hearts, both wake and sleep.
O Govinda, O Mukunda sweet,
We bow to you, at your lotus feet.

In every age, your love remains,
Binding us all in your celestial chains.
May we hear your flute in every breeze,
And feel your touch in the rustling trees.
O Krishna, lord of timeless lore,
Be with us now and forevermore.

Darshan of Banke Bihari Ji

In the heart of Vrindavan's sacred abode,
Lies a temple where divinity bestowed,
A form so charming, a sight so rare,
Banke Bihari Ji, beyond compare.
His eyes, like oceans, deep and wide,
Hold the cosmos, where love resides.
A playful smile, a blissful glow,
Enchanting hearts with a tender flow.
The veil lifts, and time stands still,
As devotees gather with hearts to fill.
Each fleeting glance, a treasure divine,
Banke Bihari Ji's grace aligns.
Peacock feathers crown his head,
A flute whispers where blessings are spread.
Adorned in silks of the brightest hue,
Radiant like the morning dew.
The bells chime softly, the crowd sways,
Lost in kirtan, in love's maze.
His darshan, a moment so sweet,
Transforms the soul, makes life complete.
Oh Banke Bihari, playful and kind,
Your image lingers in heart and mind.
Guide us always, through joy and strife,
In your presence, we find true life.

A glimpse of you, our eternal quest,
In your divine play, our spirits rest.
O Nandlal, our hearts you steer,
Forever in Vrindavan, forever near.

Krishna Janmashtami: A Divine Celebration

Under the midnight's celestial glow,
A miracle happened long ago.
In Mathura's prison, a child was born,
To banish darkness, to herald the dawn.
The heavens rejoiced; the earth stood still,
As Krishna arrived, to fulfill His will.
The thunder roared, the river made way,
To protect the one who would save the day.
A flute in hand, a smile divine,
With mischief and love, His leelas shine.
From stealing butter to lifting a hill,
He taught us faith, devotion, and will.
The Gopis danced to His melodious song,
In Vrindavan's fields, where hearts belong.
With each step, He spread delight,
Dispelling the shadows, igniting the light.
On Janmashtami, the bells resound,
Devotion in every corner is found.
Fasting, prayers, and joyful cheer,
Celebrate the Lord we hold so dear.
Oh Keshav, dear Govind, Gopal,
You teach us to rise, even when we fall.

Your life is a guide, your love a flame,
Forever we chant your glorious name.
So let us rejoice, with hearts set free,
On this blessed day of Janmashtami.
In Krishna's love, we find our way,
A path of joy, where His blessings stay.

The Eternal Love of Radha Krishna

In Vrindavan's embrace, where love feels right,
Stands Prem Mandir, glowing in divine light.
A haven where Radha and Krishna reside,
Bound by a love that time can't divide.
Marble so pure, carved with tender care,
A temple of beauty beyond compare.
Each pillar whispers their eternal song,
Of a bond unbroken, steadfast, and strong.
Radha, the heartbeat, Krishna, the soul,
Together they make the universe whole.
Her gaze reflects his endless grace,
In his flute's melody, her love finds its place.
At dusk, the temple blooms in gold,
A sight so enchanting, so lovingly told.
The chants rise high, the lamps softly gleam,
Every corner's alive with their love's dream.
Oh Prem Mandir, you cradle their tale,
Of devotion so pure, it will never pale.
Each step within feels like an embrace,
A journey to love, a sacred space.
Come, dear soul, to this temple of bliss,
Feel their love in the air, in every kiss.

In Radha Krishna's arms, let your heart stay,
And carry their affection through life's way.
For here, in this temple of devotion so deep,
Their love awakens the dreams we keep.
Oh Prem Mandir, may your beauty inspire,
A flame of love, an eternal fire.

The Digital Dawn

A world connected, by wires unseen,
Across digital paths, minds unite.
Bytes and bits build dreams so bright,
In this realm of code, we craft new light.
The hum of servers, a modern tune,
Bridging nations, under the moon.
From circuits small to AI grand,
Technology molds our future's stand.
May we wield it wisely, this mighty force,
Guiding its power on a virtuous course.
For in its hands, we place our fate,
To build or break, to love or hate.

Code Symphony

A language unseen, yet it breathes and flows,
In loops and logic, its beauty shows.
Strings of syntax, a rhythmic beat,
Code is a symphony, profound and sweet.
With every function, a story unfolds,
Logic and art, in harmony hold.
Each algorithm, a crafted tale,
Of human intellect, that shall prevail.
Beyond the lines lies a creator's mind,
Inventing worlds, one keystroke at a time.
Oh, code, the language of the modern age,
You script the world, from stage to stage.

AI's Whisper

In circuits deep, it learns and grows,
A mimic of thought, where wisdom flows.
AI's whisper, a guiding hand,
A marvel born of human command.
From data vast, it gleans the clue,
Solving riddles, creating anew.
A partner, a tool, to aid our quest,
Yet humankind must steer it best.
Let compassion guide this artificial might,
To shape a future just and bright.
For in its rise, we must remain,
The heart, the soul, the human chain.

The Internet Weaves

Threads of knowledge, vast and wide,
The internet weaves where minds reside.
From distant lands, we meet and share,
In digital space, we're always there.
But tangled too, these threads can be,
A web of truth or a false decree.
So tread with care, this boundless sea,
Seek wisdom, not just what's free.
May we use this gift with thoughtful grace,
To bridge the gaps in time and space.
For in its reach, the world's unite,
A tool of change, both day and night.

Eternal Love

Under the Kadamba, where rivers sing,
Radha and Krishna, in love's eternal spring.
Their laughter echoes, their eyes entwined,
A bond divine, in hearts enshrined.
The flute's melody, soft and sweet,
Draws Radha close, where their souls meet.
In every moment, their story unfolds,
A timeless love, the universe holds.
May we find, in their sacred lore,
A path to love, forevermore.
Radha Krishna, guide our way,
In your embrace, we long to stay.

The Dance of Divinity

The moonlight glows, the forest sways,
In Vrindavan's heart, where devotion lays.
Radha and Krishna, in a dance divine,
Their love transcends the bounds of time.
Every step, a celestial art,
Echoing deeply in every heart.
The Gopis' joy, the universe sings,
As Krishna's flute to Radha clings.
Oh, sacred dance, oh, love so pure,
In your rhythm, all souls endure.
Teach us to love, without bounds or fear,
In Radha Krishna, forever near.

Flute of the Heart

The melody plays, soft and true,
Krishna's flute calls out to you.
Its tune a whisper, a sacred sound,
Binding all in love profound.
Radha listens, her heart in flight,
Drawn to him under the starlit night.
In every note, the world finds peace,
In every chord, all worries cease.
Oh Krishna, play forevermore,
Your flute's sweet song we all adore.
A guide, a balm, a soul's delight,
Your music leads us to the light.

Vrindavan's Eternal Bliss

In Vrindavan's grove, where love takes form,
Radha and Krishna weather the storm.
Their eyes meet, their hearts align,
In the realm of love, truly divine.
Each petal blooms in their sacred name,
The forest sings their eternal fame.
A love untouched by space or time,
Echoed in chants, in prose, and rhyme.
May we wander where their feet have trod,
Seeking the path of love to God.
In Vrindavan's grace, we find our way,
To eternal bliss, where hearts shall stay.

The Stillness Within

In the quiet, the soul takes flight,
Through the veil of dark into the light.
Breath by breath, the noise subsides,
The heart awakens, where peace resides.
The storms of thought, they fade away,
In the calm of this sacred stay.
A journey inward, vast and deep,
Where the soul finds rest, the spirit sleeps.
Oh, meditation, your gift divine,
A bridge to the eternal, a steady line.
May we sit in your grace each day,
And find the light to guide our way.

A Moment of Zen

The world may rush, but time stands still,
In the space of quiet, the heart can fill.
Each breath a step, each thought a stream,
Flowing gently, like a dream.
In meditation's arms, the chaos fades,
A temple of calm the mind invades.
With closed eyes, the journey begins,
A sacred dance of silence within.
Oh, zenful state, so pure, so true,
Through you, we're born, completely anew.
May we cherish this gift so rare,
And find ourselves, fully aware.

Healing Vibrations

The bowl sings softly, its tone so clear,
A symphony of peace, for hearts to hear.
Each sound a ripple through the soul,
Mending the broken, making us whole.
The gong's deep hum, a timeless call,
A wave of calm, embracing all.
In sound, we heal; in tone, we grow,
A harmony only the spirit can know.
Let these vibrations, ancient and wise,
Guide us gently to tranquil skies.
Oh, sound of solace, oh, healing tune,
Lift our spirits, like a crescent moon.

The Symphony of Peace

A melody floats, unseen yet near,
Drawing away every shadow of fear.
Each tone a whisper, a soothing guide,
Reaching the places where pain resides.
The drumbeat echoes, the heart aligns,
With rhythms ancient, transcending time.
Through bowls and gongs, the spirit flows,
Where healing lives and love bestows.
In sound, we find the strength to be,
A soul at peace, calm and free.
Oh, symphony bright, a healer's art,
Forever etched within the heart.

Resonance of Love

The bell chimes gently; its call so sweet,
A resonance of love, in every beat.
Its echoes linger, its tones repair,
Filling the silence with love and care.
Each vibration a sacred embrace,
Filling the soul with healing grace.
The sound unfolds, the heart it warms,
Breaking through life's chaotic storms.
Oh, resonance pure, oh, loving sound,
In your rhythm, peace is found.
May your music forever remain,
A guide to joy, through every pain.

A Bride's Heart

Today I stand, draped in red and gold,
A story begins, a new chapter unfolds.
With every bangle, with every thread,
Dreams and blessings gently spread.
The anklets chime with a joyful tune,
The stars bear witness, the radiant moon.
Eyes glisten with love, with hope so true,
As I step forward, my world feels new.
A blend of laughter, of tears and grace,
Leaving behind my familiar place.
To a home unknown, with hearts to meet,
Carrying love, my journey's complete.
The vows we take, the fire's warm glow,
Promises eternal, as rivers flow.
Two souls unite, two hearts align,
A bond as sacred, as old as time.
Oh, my heart flutters, a gentle ache,
For the ties I leave, for the steps I take.
Yet in this union, I find my part,
A world of love, a bride's full heart.

The Enchanting Beauty of Sikkim

Nestled beneath the Himalayan sky,
Where snow-capped peaks reach up high.
Sikkim, a gem of serene delight,
A paradise wrapped in nature's light.
The Kanchenjunga stands so proud,
Cloaked in mist, a heavenly shroud.
Its valleys echo with streams that sing,
Through lush green meadows, life takes wing.
Orchids bloom in colors rare,
Filling the air with fragrances fair.
The Rhododendrons paint the trails,
As mountain breezes tell their tales.
Gurudongmar's waters, pure and still,
Reflect the heavens, the mountains' will.
And Tsomgo Lake, a mirrored charm,
Nestled in nature's gentle arms.
The monasteries hum with prayers so deep,
A soulful calm, a spiritual keep.
Prayer flags flutter in the mountain breeze,
Whispering peace through the forested trees.
Oh Sikkim, land of tranquil grace,
You hold the earth in a warm embrace.
A beauty untouched, a dream so true,
Sikkim, our hearts belong to you.

Snowfall in Solang Valley

In Solang Valley, where dreams unfold,
A winter wonderland, pure and cold.
The heavens weep with flakes of white,
Draping the earth in a frosty light.
The mountains gleam in a silken sheen,
A tranquil realm, serene and pristine.
Each tree stands tall in a crystal cloak,
Whispering tales as the silence spoke.
Snowflakes dance in the gentle breeze,
Kissing the valley, embracing the trees.
A quiet magic fills the air,
A world transformed, beyond compare.
Laughter rings as skiers glide,
Children play on the snowy tide.
The valley hums with joy untold,
In Solang's arms, memories unfold.
Oh, snowfall fair, your beauty stays,
In Solang's heart, through winter's gaze.
A land of wonder, soft and bright,
A snowy dream in purest light.

Stepping Into New Horizons

A new door opens, a path untold,
A journey begins, fresh and bold.
With dreams alight and hopes in tow,
The thrill of learning begins to grow.
The desk awaits, the team stands near,
A world of challenges, bright and clear.
Every task feels like a treasure to find,
Igniting the spark within my mind.
The nervous flutter, the eager grin,
A chapter starts where I begin.
Building bridges, crafting my way,
Turning each effort into a brighter day.
Oh, the thrill of a brand-new start,
Fills my soul, ignites my heart.
Here's to the journey, the dreams I'll weave,
With every step, a mark I'll leave.

A Dream Called Home

Brick by brick, a dream takes flight,
A haven born from hope's delight.
A place to call my very own,
A sanctuary, a seed I've sown.
The keys in hand, the door swings wide,
A world awaits on the other side.
Each room whispers, "Here you'll grow,"
With love and care, its warmth will show.
The walls will echo laughter and tears,
The stories of life through fleeting years.
From quiet nights to mornings bright,
This home will cradle joy and light.
Oh, the pride, the peace, the thrill,
To shape a space with heart and will.
My own four walls, my sacred space,
A lifelong dream, now in its place.
Here I'll build, here I'll stay,
In my own home, come what may.
A treasure cherished, forever true,
A dream fulfilled, a life anew.

Happiness in Every Journey

A suitcase packed, a heart set free,
The open road calls out to me.
Mountains high and oceans wide,
Happiness blooms where wonders reside.
The thrill of places yet unknown,
Each step a story, a seed I've sown.
With every sunrise, a new start,
Travel awakens the soul and heart.
Through winding paths and bustling streets,
In every face, a tale it meets.
The joy of freedom, the world's embrace,
In every moment, a treasure to trace.
Oh, how sweet this journey feels,
A joy that time itself reveals.
In travel's arms, my spirit flies,
Happiness found beneath open skies.

The Peace of Singing Bowl Meditation

A gentle chime, a sacred sound,
Ripples of peace that softly surround.
The singing bowl hums, its tones take flight,
Guiding the soul to a tranquil light.
With every note, the chaos fades,
A calmness blooms, the storm abates.
The resonance whispers, ancient and wise,
Awakening peace beneath closed eyes.
The body rests, the spirit ascends,
In these vibrations, the heart mends.
Each echo heals, each tone aligns,
A symphony of love that deeply shines.
Oh, singing bowl, your voice so pure,
A balm for the soul, a timeless cure.
In your melody, the world's still grace,
Meditation finds its peaceful place.

Workplace Bonds

In the hum of work, where hours blend,
Blooms the joy of a colleague, a friend.
Amid the tasks and the daily grind,
A kindred spirit, a heart aligned.
With shared laughter and coffee breaks,
A bond of trust and joy it makes.
In whispered chats or a helping hand,
Office friendships forever stand.
Through deadlines tight and pressures steep,
Together we climb, together we leap.
A cheer, a nudge, a moment to share,
An unspoken promise, always there.
Oh, friendships formed where work resides,
A treasure rare that life provides.
For in the bustle, they bring the light,
Making the office a place so bright.

My Happy Place: My Husband's Nest

In the chaos of life, where moments stray,
Your arms are the haven where I long to stay.
A nest so warm, a love so true,
My happy place is always with you.
Your laughter rings like a gentle song,
In your embrace, I feel I belong.
Through every storm, your strength prevails,
A shelter of love, where no fear trails.
Your touch, a balm, your voice, my guide,
With you, my heart finds joy inside.
In your nest, the world fades away,
A place of peace, where I wish to stay.
Oh, my husband, my soul's sweet rest,
In your love, I am truly blessed.
For in your arms, life feels its best,
My happy place, my husband's nest.